A true story from the Bible

# DANIEL
## and the very
# HUNGRY
# LIONS

· WRITTEN BY ·
Tim Thornborough

· ILLUSTRATED BY ·
Jennifer Davison

Some books you just listen to as someone else reads them. But this book is different.

Every time there is a word on the page that is a sound, you have to try and make the sound yourself.

Shall we practise the sound a lion makes?

# ROAR!
# ROOOAR!
# ROOOOOOOAR!

Now we're ready to start this true story from the Bible about a man called Daniel, a king called Darius, and some VERY hungry lions.

Daniel and the Very Hungry Lions © The Good Book Company, 2019. Reprinted 2020, 2021, 2022, 2023. Words by Tim Thornborough. Illustrations by Jennifer Davison. Design and art direction by André Parker
thegoodbook.co.uk • thegoodbook.com • thegoodbook.com.au • thegoodbook.co.nz • thegoodbook.co.in
ISBN: 9781784983321. Printed in India

Every day the people of Babylon woke up to the sound of the king's roaring, ravenous lions.

ROAR!
ROAR!
GNASH
GNASH

And every day Daniel got out of bed, went to the window, knelt down and prayed to God.

Daniel loved God and talked to him each and every day. Daniel trusted God and knew that he was in control of everything that happened.

CLICK
CLICK

God had made Daniel wise and clever and honest.

King Darius liked Daniel and put him in charge.

SCRATCH
SCRATCH

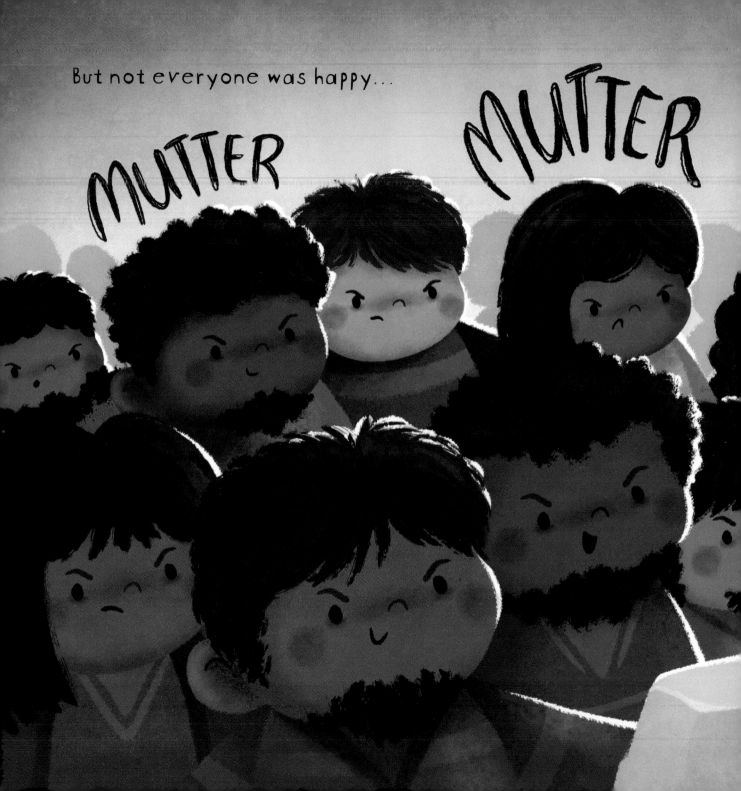

PLOT PLOT

Some important men didn't like Daniel.
They wanted to get rid of him.

What would they do?

They came up with
a clever, clever plan.

"Oh great king! You must
make a law that can
never be broken.

Anyone who prays to
God must be fed to the
roaring, ravenous lions."

GROVEL
GROVEL

King Darius agreed. And he made a law that could not be broken.

What should Daniel do?

Daniel Loved God. Daniel served God. Daniel knew that God was in control.

THiNK THiNK

He knew that God could be trusted – even if he was thrown to the roaring, ravenous lions.

SCRATCH SCRATCH

So each and every day he went to his window, knelt down and carried on praying to God.

What do you think happened next?

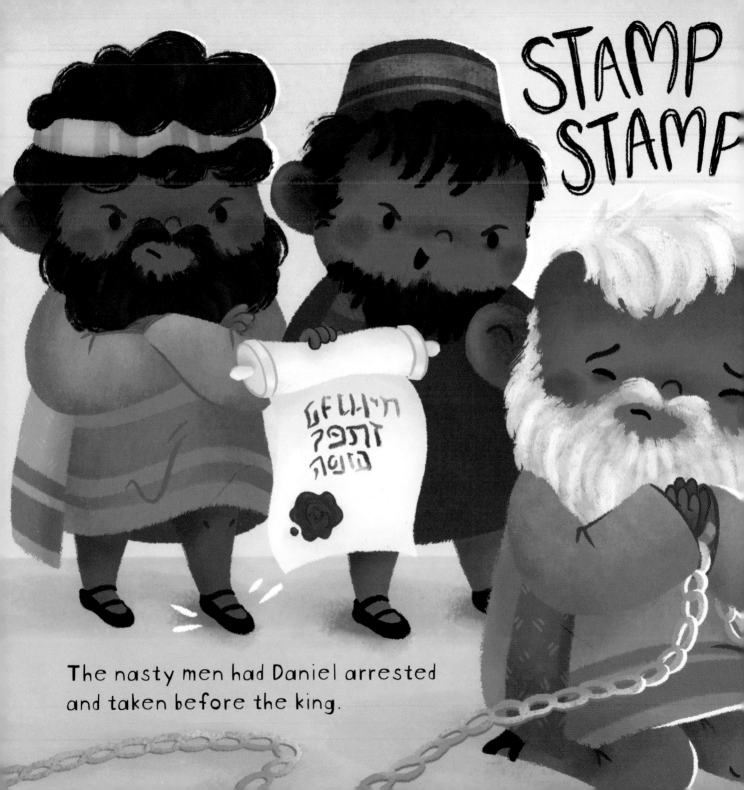

STAMP
STAMP

The nasty men had Daniel arrested and taken before the king.

King Darius was sad.
He knew he had
been tricked.

He didn't want to
feed Daniel to the
roaring, ravenous lions,
but he had made a law
that could not be broken.

# CLINK CLINK

What could he do?

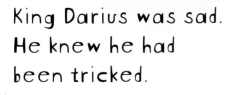

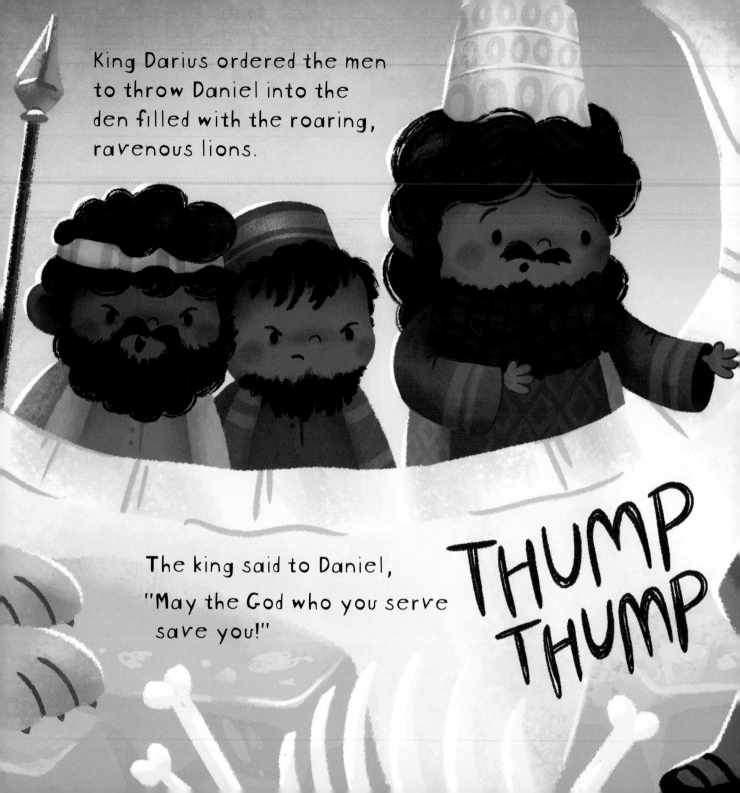

King Darius ordered the men to throw Daniel into the den filled with the roaring, ravenous lions.

The king said to Daniel, "May the God who you serve save you!"

THUMP THUMP

# BUMP
# BUMP

A great big stone was put over the entrance, and all went quiet.

What would the lions do?

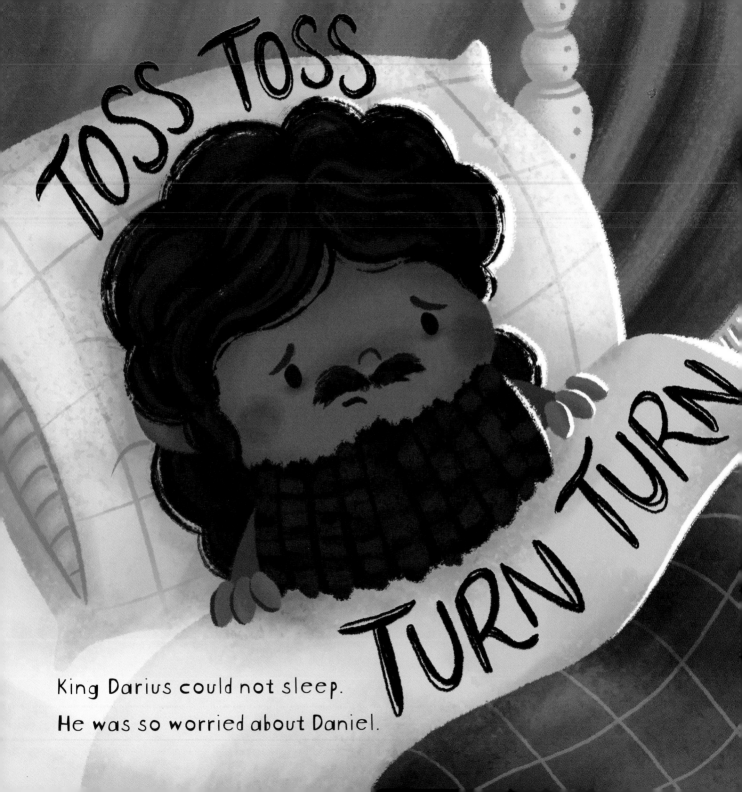

TOSS TOSS

TURN TURN

King Darius could not sleep.
He was so worried about Daniel.

And he was cross that he had been tricked.

Would God keep Daniel safe from the roaring, ravenous lions?

What do you think?

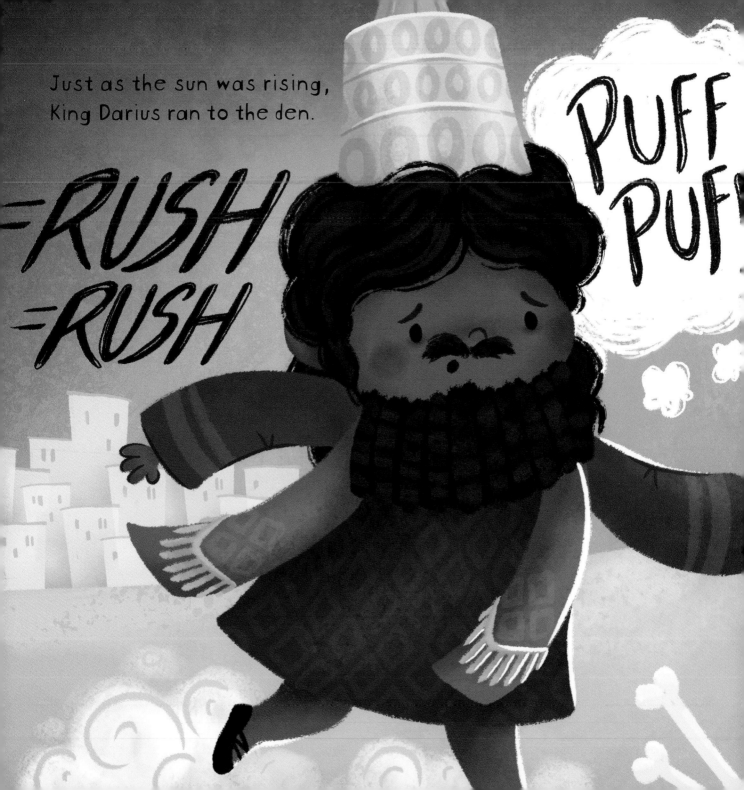

He called out, "Daniel – are you there?
Did God save you from the roaring, ravenous lions?"

"YES!"
CALLED DANIEL

"God sent an angel who
shut their mouths!"

The stone was rolled away,
and Daniel came out alive and well.

There was not a single scratch on him!

"Now where are those evil men who tricked me?" said Darius.

What would the king do?

He ordered his men to throw
them into the den...

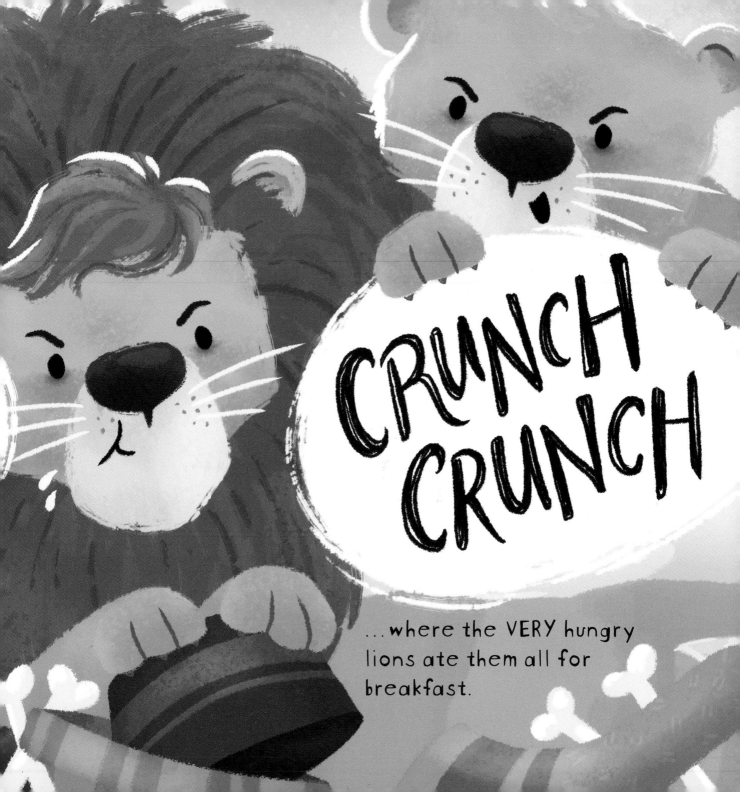

CRUNCH CRUNCH

...where the VERY hungry lions ate them all for breakfast.

King Darius learned
something important
that day.

He told EVERYONE
in his kingdom...

"The God that Daniel loves
and serves...

the God who rescued
Daniel from the
roaring, ravenous lions...

is the one true God who lives
for ever!"